M. **.D.**

I WILL;

BE THOU CLEAN...

BOOK OF HEALING

(Quiero; Sé Limpio...Libro De Sanidad)

And behold, there came a leper and worshiped Him, saying, "Lord, if Thou wilt, Thou canst make me clean." And Jesus put forth His hand and touched him, saying, "I will: be thou clean." And immediately his leprosy was cleansed.

Matthew 8:2–3

TRILOGY

Trilogy Christian Publishers

A Wholly Owned Subsidiary of Trinity Broadcasting Network

2442 Michelle Drive
Tustin, CA 92780

I WILL; BE THOU CLEAN...BOOK OF HEALING

For information, address Trilogy Christian Publishing

Rights Department, 2442 Michelle Drive, Tustin, Ca 92780.

Manufactured in the United States of America

10 9 8 7 6 5 4 3 2 1

Library of Congress Cataloging-in-Publication Data is available.

ISBN 979-8-88738-421-4

ISBN 979-8-88738-422-1 (ebook)

DEDICATION

This book is dedicated to God, who gave me the revelation to write it. It is also dedicated to my sons, Daniel and René, my family, and each person God had in mind when He instructed me to write it.

Thank you, Lord

ACKNOWLEDGMENTS

First, I would like to thank my God, who placed this book in my heart and has given me the privilege to write it. I am also thankful for my sons Daniel and René. Thank you, Daniel, for all the time spent on the computer and you, René, for creating the cover of this book.

Also, I would like to thank everyone who in one way or another helped in the editorial process. Thank you Rosa Acevedo, Omayra Medina, Milagros Domínguez, Sonia Mendoza, Margarita Machado, Nodelis Figueroa. A special thanks to Vanessa Barreto: you are a vessel of honor used by the Lord. Thank you for your friendship, your time, and your motivation. God bless you, now and always.

May you all be greatly blessed.

CONTENTS

CHAPTER ONE

WHAT SOME CHRISTIANS BELIEVE ABOUT SICKNESS

... and I will take sickness away from the midst of thee.

Exodus 23:25

Today, many Christians are living with illness. Many of them believe sickness comes from God. Therefore, they accept illness as part of God's plan and suffer because they want to obey His Word and be humbly at His service. They believe God's will is for them to be sick. However, the Word of God says that He came to give us life, abundant life.

Terminal illnesses such as cancer and *AIDS* bring pain and death, slowly destroying a person's life. Having cancer or *AIDS* or any illness does not in any way represent the abundant life promised by God. Furthermore, when God created the earth, He did not create sickness. If we look and the first chapter of Genesis, we notice that everything God created was very good. Let's look at the creation:

> *And God saw everything that He had made, and behold, it was very good...*
>
> Genesis 1:31

God not only created good things, everything He created was *very* good. If sickness were the work of God, He would have included it in His creation. Sickness is *NOT* from God.

Still others believe that sickness is a test from God. God does not need to test anyone because He knows what each person will do. Thinking of God in this manner is equal to believing in a limited God who has to resort to sickness to achieve His purpose in our lives. God knows everything; He knows how we are going to react to any type of adversity, so He does not need to make us sick in order to know what we are going to do. God wants you healthy; He paid the price. Where? On Mount Calvary:

> *But He was wounded for our transgressions; He was bruised for our iniquities. The chastisement of our peace was upon Him, and with His stripes we are healed.*
>
> Isaiah 53:5

To think that God brings us sickness is to think that He tempts us. God does not test or tempt anyone. Let's look at His Word:

> *Let no man say when he is tempted, "I am tempted by God;" for God cannot be tempted with evil, neither tempteth He any man.*
>
> James 1:13

Temptation is the work of Satan; the tests come from the devil. The devil even tempted Jesus Christ:

> *Then was Jesus led up by the Spirit into the wilderness to be tempted by the devil. And when He had fasted forty days and forty nights, He afterward hungered. And when the tempter came to Him, he said, "If Thou be the Son of God, command that these stones be made bread."*
>
> Matthew 4:1–3

Nowhere in the Bible does it say that God tempted anyone. The Bible clearly presents to us the true tempter, namely the devil.

In Luke 11:14–18 we see the explanation Jesus Christ himself gives to the Pharisees about temptation. The Pharisees, upon seeing Christ's miracle, said it was because He had driven out the demons through Beelzebub (the prince of the demons). Jesus explains to them that Satan cannot survive when divided against himself.

Let's look at this:

And He was casting out a demon, and it was mute. And it came to pass when the demon had gone out, the mute one spoke; and the people wondered. But some of them said, "He casteth out devils through Beelzebub, the chief of the demons. And others, testing Him, sought from Him a sign from Heaven. But He, knowing their thoughts, said unto them, "Every kingdom divided against itself is brought to desolation; and a house divided against a house falleth. If Satan also be divided against himself, how shall his kingdom stand—because ye say that I cast out devils through Beelzebub?"

Luke 11:14–18

In other words, they said Satan summons the demon of sickness and then removes it. That is absurd. No wrongdoer steals from a person, then returns to them what they stole, and no one takes a prisoner only to release them later. God is the healer; God is the liberator.

Other Christians believe that God is glorified in sickness. Throughout the Bible, we read that God is glorified in salvation, in health, in liberation, and in the forgiveness of our sins. The woman who suffered from bleeding for twelve years did not glorify God until she received health. During the twelve years of her illness, she did not glorify the power of God. And the Bible narrates her cure, not her submission in this illness, because God is glorified by health. The man who was born blind did not glorify God during his life as a blind man, but when he received sight. The lepers whom God cured glorified Him when they became clean. Bartimaeus, the blind man, glorified God when he received sight.

In John 11:40, Jesus was going to raise Lazarus from the dead. He said to Martha: "Said I not unto thee that if thou would believe, thou should see the glory of God?" Jesus was going to resurrect Lazarus. Jesus would defeat death, giving life to Lazarus. Thus, life glorifies God, and health is life.

Let's look at times when God is glorified.

The Parable of the Ten Lepers:

And one of them when he saw that he was healed, turned back and with a loud voice glorified God.

Luke 17:15

Another blind man:

And immediately he received his sight and followed Him, glorifying God. And all the people, when they saw it, gave praise unto God.

Luke 18:43

There are people who believe God has punished them for their sins and are therefore not worthy of God's healing. But if you are a child of God, washed in the blood of the Lamb, that blood will cleanse you of all sin and free you from evil. Don't play the role of the victim; Christ paid the price on Mount Calvary for your sins, your healing, and your salvation.

We know that God is our father; we know that He loves us. What father would give their child cancer or *AIDS* to bring them to obedience? No one who loves their children would do so; least of all God, as God is *LOVE.*

Herein is love: not that we loved God, but that He loved us and sent His Son to be the propitiation for our sins.

1 John 4:10

If God is love, a perfect love does not wish any harm to their children. Furthermore, if He sent His son to grant us forgiveness and eternal life by paying with His life, He didn't do this to make us suffer. He loved us first, long before being born, regardless of our sins.

> *In this was manifested the love of God toward us: that God sent His only begotten Son into the world that we might live through Him.*
>
> 1 John 4:9

If living means being free of illness, if God in His infinite mercy sent His Son so that we could live, He cannot contradict Himself and wish illness on His children. Remember:

> *...I am come that they might have life, and that they might have it more abundantly.*
>
> John 10:10

I am a mother and I am not better than God; how can I say that God gives us sickness? If I, with my limited love, would not give my children sickness, how could God, who is the perfect love, give cancer to His children? When Christians accept these things as truths, they are accepting sickness. They are choosing death of their own free will. Deuteronomy 30:19 says:

> *I call heaven and earth to record this day against you that I have set before you life and death, blessing and cursing. Therefore choose life, that both thou and thy seed may live.*

Notice that God Himself suggests that we should choose life, and choosing life is being in good health. But in choosing sickness, we are choosing the curse and we are choosing death.

God gave us free will and respectfully accepts our decision to live in sickness. God is not going to break your free will; if you choose to live in sickness, He must accept it. When people make this choice, they are distancing themselves from the only thing that can heal them. And that is the devil's trap: to make you believe sickness comes from God and distance you from the healer so that you will die. Remember, God came to give us life, LIFE IN ABUNDANCE.

Imagine how surprised these Christians would feel when, upon reaching heaven, they asked God for an explanation of why He sent them *AIDS*. What do you think God's answer would be? "My child, you took for granted the sacrifice on the cross. I gave up my life so that you could live, and you chose death. On Mount Calvary, I suffered sickness so that you did not have to bear it; there I paid the price for your health and you chose illness."

> *Surely He hath borne our griefs and carried our sorrows; yet we did esteem Him stricken, smitten of God, and afflicted.*
>
> Isaiah 53:4

CHAPTER TWO

GOD'S WILL IS TO HEAL YOU

Behold, I will bring it health and cure; and I will cure them and will reveal unto them the abundance of peace and truth.

Jeremiah 33:6

The Word says "I will cure them," not "I will make them sick;" it says that He will bring medicine or cure, not illness. As far as I know, medicine is meant to cure. God is not going to make us sick to heal us later; that would make God imperfect. Furthermore, God does not know sickness Himself, so He cannot give what He does not have; much less contradict His own word.

In Romans 12:2, the Word tells us what God wills for His people:

And be not conformed to this world, but be ye transformed by the renewing of your mind, that ye may prove what is that good and acceptable and perfect will of God.

Let us analyze this verse. First, sickness is not good, and no one in their right mind likes to feel bad; nor is having cancer or *AIDS* a pleasant thing. Second, sickness is not perfect because it limits us. God is a perfect God, therefore God cannot give us what He does not have. God does not know sickness, nor did He create it. Illness is not pleasant; ask anyone who is in the hospital if being sick is pleasant. God is perfect, and everything He created was indeed "very good." (Genesis 1:31).

God did not create sickness because everything He created was good. Sickness is a consequence of man's disobedience; that's when sickness appeared, as a result of the curse. God's will is to heal you, so much so that He has given us power and authority over illness.

Mark 16:18 says:

> *...they shall take up serpents, and if they drink any deadly thing, it shall not hurt them. They shall lay hands on the sick, and they shall recover.*

That is God's will—for believers to lay their hands on the sick and heal them. If God sent His disciples (as well as us, His believers) and gave them power over foul spirits so that they could cast them out and heal sickness and disease, He would not give believers power over sickness and at the same time give them sickness; this would be an insane God. This mandate was for all believers, since God does not make exceptions, making some people sick and giving others the power to heal the sick.

> *Heal the sick, cleanse the lepers, raise the dead, cast out devils. Freely ye have received; freely give.*
>
> Matthew 10:8

If we receive freely, sickness does not come from God's grace. When we receive the power to heal, God gives all of us believers the authority to do so. Otherwise, He would be making exceptions with people, and God does not make these exceptions.

> *For there is no respect of persons with God.*
>
> Romans 2:11

To say that God gives sickness is equal to saying and believing that God is unfair. God is a fair judge and His judgments are perfect. God does not contradict Himself in His Word. If God gives us the power to heal, God does not want people to be sick. Otherwise, He would not have given us the power to heal the sick.

The Word also says:

> *Every good gift and every perfect gift is from above, and cometh down from the Father of lights, with whom is no variableness, neither shadow of turning.*
>
> James 1:17

Sickness is not a good gift, much less a perfect talent. If we look at the Scriptures, we realize that God never rejected anyone for being sick; He healed everyone.

> *And Jesus went about all Galilee, teaching in their synagogues and preaching the Gospel of the Kingdom, and healing all manner of sickness and all manner of disease among the people.*
>
> Matthew 4:23

> *And Jesus went forth and saw a great multitude, and was moved with compassion toward them, and He healed their sick.*
>
> Matthew 14:14

> *And great multitudes followed Him, and He healed them there.*
>
> Matthew 19:2

He healed them all. He rejected no one, and these words are as valid today as they were 2000 years ago; Christ continues to heal, since He is the same today and forever.

> *Jesus Christ is the same yesterday, and today, and forever.*
>
> Hebrews 13:8

His Word does not change.

Verily I say unto you, this generation shall not pass till all these things be fulfilled. Heaven and earth shall pass away, but My Words shall not pass away.

Matthew 24:34–35

CHAPTER THREE

CHRIST'S VICTORY OVER SICKNESS

Who His own self bore our sins in His own body on the tree, that we, being dead to sins, should live unto righteousness; by whose stripes ye were healed.

Peter 2:24

The only place where Christ received sickness was on Mount Calvary, so that you and I would not get sick. There, just as He paid for our sins, He paid the price for our healing.

Surely He hath borne our griefs and carried our sorrows; yet we did esteem Him stricken, smitten of God, and afflicted.

Isaiah 53:4

But He was wounded for our transgressions; He was bruised for our iniquities. The chastisement of our peace was upon Him, and with His stripes we are healed.

Isaiah 53:5

That it might be fulfilled which was spoken by Isaiah the prophet, who said, "He Himself took our infirmities and bore our sicknesses.

Matthew 8:17

God made man, and as an unblemished Lamb, He bore the full weight of our faults so that we could be free of sin. In the same way that He bore sin, He who had no sin, He also bore sickness,

He who knew no sickness. His only purpose for doing so was that we would not have to bear it. Jesus Christ overcame sickness so that you and I would not have to suffer it. To receive sickness as something coming from God is saying that Christ's sacrifice on the cross was not enough.

"And by His wounds we were healed." This is God's promise and God's Word; and it has been done, as it is in the past tense. The Word does not say that you will be healed; it says that before we were born, God had paid the price for sickness, be it a common cold or *AIDS*. All this God did through His Son so that you and I could walk in health.

CHAPTER FOUR

JESUS CHRIST: A PERFECT MODEL OF HEALTH

Be ye therefore perfect, even as your Father who is in Heaven is perfect.

Matthew 5:48

In 1 Corinthians 11:1, we read: *Be ye followers of me, even as I also am of Christ.* Nowhere in the Bible is there a sick Jesus Christ. God is a healthy, perfect God, and we need to imitate that perfection. The only place where Christ took sickness was on Mount Calvary, so that we did not have to take it. Just as He bore our sins, being an unblemished Lamb, He also bore sickness so that we would not have to bear it. Let us obey the word and imitate Christ, imitate His health, as the Bible presents us with a God who is perfect and healthy.

If God would have wanted us to live in sickness, He would not have paid the price He paid. We were bought with blood.

For ye are bought with a price. Therefore glorify God in your body and in your spirit, which are God's.

1 Corinthians 6:20

If we were bought with blood, it was so that we could live in health, not in sickness. To glorify God in our bodies, we need to be healthy; a sick person is never a testimony to the life of God. Only the healthy glorify God in their bodies. If our body is God's and God is perfect, we must walk in that perfection. We are of God, His making, and if that is so, we cannot walk in sickness, but rather in health. How can a sick person glorify God in a sick body? What God do we serve? Philippians 3:17 says, "*Brethren, be followers together of me, and mark those who so walk, as ye have us for an example."* We are examples of Christ and many will imitate that example; we cannot be sick if others are to imitate us; we need to enjoy good health so that others enjoy it.

And ye became followers of us and of the Lord, having received the Word in much affliction, with the joy of the Holy Ghost.

1 Thessalonians 1:6

We are imitators of His perfect health. Christ never stopped preaching because He got sick. Let's imitate Him.

Be ye therefore followers of God, as dear children.

Ephesians 5:1

If we are His beloved children and we enjoy good health, then Christ gave us victory over sickness so that we would live in health.

For God so loved the world that He gave His only begotten Son, that whosoever believeth in Him should not perish, but have everlasting life.

John 3:16

Let's look at other examples of His perfection in the Word:

As for God, His way is perfect...

Psalm 18:30

There is no sickness in His way.

It is God that girdeth me with strength, and maketh my way perfect.

Psalm 18:32

If my way is perfect, there can be no sickness in it, as He who created me is perfect and was never sick.

Be ye therefore perfect, even as your Father who is in Heaven is perfect.

Matthew 5:48

One of the requirements of perfection is to live in health.

Until we all come into the unity of the faith and of the knowledge of the Son of God, unto a perfect man, unto the measure of the stature of the fullness of Christ.

Ephesians 33:13

Him we preach, warning every man and teaching every man in all wisdom, that we may present every man perfect in Christ Jesus.

Colossians 1:28

Epaphras, a servant of Christ who is one of you, saluteth you, always laboring fervently for you in prayers, that ye may stand perfect and complete in all the will of God.

Colossians 4:12

...that the man of God may be perfect, thoroughly equipped for all good works.

2 Timothy 3:17

In order to be a perfect man or woman, we cannot be sick. We have to walk in health as Christ walked. Part of preparing for good works is being in good health.

But let patience have her perfect work, that ye may be perfect and entire, lacking nothing.

James 1:4

To be perfect and entire and lacking nothing, we have to live in health. That is God's perfection in us.

CHAPTER FIVE

HEALING IN THE GOSPELS

And Jesus went about all Galilee, teaching in their synagogues and preaching the Gospel of the Kingdom, and healing all manner of sickness and all manner of disease among the people.

Matthew 4:23

And His fame went throughout all Syria. And they brought unto Him all sick people who were taken with divers diseases and torments, and those who were possessed with devils, and those who were lunatic, and those who had the palsy; and He healed them.

Matthew 4:24

And behold, there came a leper and worshiped Him, saying, "Lord, if Thou wilt, Thou canst make me clean." And Jesus put forth His hand and touched him, saying, "I will: be thou clean." And immediately his leprosy was cleansed.

Matthew 8:2–3

Jesus did not say, "keep your leprosy, it is a test." Without giving it a second thought, He healed him. Jesus did not say that His Father's will was for him to be sick, as our Father's will is for us to live in health. Nor did He say that His sickness would glorify God. God cannot give what He does not have; He is a perfect God who does not know sickness, and His health is perfect.

And when Jesus had entered into Capernaum, there came unto Him a centurion, beseeching Him and saying, "Lord, my servant lieth at home sick with the palsy and grievously tormented." And Jesus said unto him, "I will come and heal him."

JESUS WANTS TO HEAL YOU

The centurion answered and said, "Lord, I am not worthy that Thou shouldest come under my roof. But speak the word only, and my servant shall be healed. For I am a man under authority, having soldiers under me. And I say to this man, 'Go!' and he goeth; and to another, 'Come!' and he cometh; and to my servant, 'Do this!' and he doeth it." When Jesus heard it, He marveled and said to those who followed,

"Verily I say unto you, I have not found such great faith, no, not in Israel. And I say unto you, that many shall come from the east and west, and shall sit down with Abraham and Isaac and Jacob in the Kingdom of Heaven. But the children of the kingdom shall be cast out into outer darkness: there shall be weeping and gnashing of teeth." And Jesus said unto the centurion, "Go thy way, and as thou hast believed, so be it done unto thee." And his servant was healed in that selfsame hour."

Matthew 8:5–13

In this story, Jesus healed the servant based on the centurion's faith, by sending His word. He did not even have to see the servant or place His hands on him. *JESUS HEALED HIM*. Jesus sent His word and that word is with us *TODAY*. The same word that healed the leper, the same word that healed the centurion's servant is current today because *Jesus Christ is the same yesterday, and today, and forever* (Hebrews 13:8).

Peter's mother-in-law did not ask to be healed, yet Jesus healed her.

And when Jesus had come into Peter's house, He saw his wife' mother lying and sick with a fever. And He touched her hand, and the fever left her, and she arose and ministered unto them.

Matthew 8:14–15

When the evening had come, they brought unto Him many who were possessed with devils, and He cast out the spirits with His word and healed all who were sick.

Matthew 8:16

The Bible says He healed *ALL WHO WERE SICK*; God does not make exceptions with people. God did not ask them if they were sinners or not, He simply healed them.

...that it might be fulfilled which was spoken by Isaiah the prophet, who said, "He Himself took our infirmities and bore our sicknesses."

Matthew 8:17

And behold, they brought to Him a man sick with the palsy, lying on a bed. And Jesus, seeing their faith, said unto the one sick with the palsy, "Son, be of good cheer; thy sins be forgiven thee. And behold, certain of the scribes said within themselves, "This man blasphemeth. And Jesus, knowing their thoughts, said, "Why think ye evil in your hearts? For which is easier: to say, 'Thy sins be forgiven thee,' or to say, 'Arise and walk' But that ye may know that the Son of Man hath power on earth to forgive sins,"— (then said He to the one sick with palsy) "Arise, take up thy bed and go unto thine house." And he arose and departed to his house.

Matthew 9:2–7

While He spoke these things unto them, behold, there came a certain ruler and worshiped Him, saying, "My daughter is even now dead, but come and lay Thy hand upon her, and she shall live." And Jesus arose and followed him, and so did His disciples.

Matthew 9:18–19

And behold, a woman who was diseased with an issue of blood for twelve years came up behind Him and touched the hem of His garment; for she said to herself, "If I may but touch His garment, I shall be whole. But Jesus turned about, and when He saw her, He said, "Daughter, be of good comfort; thy faith hath made thee whole. And the woman was made whole from that hour.

Matthew 9:20–22

The word *whole* also means healthy, therefore the woman received healing in that moment. The key was her faith, which Jesus acknowledges and because of it heals her. The Word says that for him who believes, everything is possible. She believed and was healed. You can also believe and be healed.

And when Jesus came into the ruler's house and saw the minstrels and the people making a noise, He said unto them, "Give way, for the maid is not dead, but sleepeth." And they laughed Him to scorn.

Matthew 9:23–24

Before the eyes of these people, Jesus was insane. Everyone there had seen the girl die, and now this man comes in and says she is only sleeping. Jesus did not care, but He cast them out because of their lack of faith.

But when the people were put outside, He went in and took her by the hand, and the maid arose.

Matthew 9:25

Dear brother or sister, the girl was dead and Jesus brought her back to life; you, in turn, are alive; regardless of any condition, you are alive. No matter how bad you feel or how sick you are, God wants to heal you.

And Jesus went about all Galilee, teaching in their synagogues and preaching the Gospel of the Kingdom, and healing all manner of sickness and all manner of disease among the people.

Matthew 9:35

And great multitudes came unto Him, having with them those who were lame, blind, dumb, maimed, and many others, and cast them down at Jesus' feet, and He healed them.

Matthew 15:30

Insomuch that the multitude wondered when they saw the dumb to speak, and the maimed to be whole, the lame to walk, and the blind to see. And they glorified the God of Israel.

Matthew 15:31

And behold, two blind men were sitting by the wayside when they heard that Jesus was passing by, and they cried out, saying, "Have mercy on us, O Lord, Thou Son of David!" And the multitude rebuked them, that they should hold their peace; but they cried out the more, saying, "Have mercy on us, O Lord, Thou Son of David!" And Jesus stood still, and called them and said, "What will ye that I shall do unto you?" They said unto Him, "Lord, that our eyes may be opened." So Jesus had compassion on them and touched their eyes, and immediately their eyes received sight, and they followed Him.

Matthew 20:30–34

In the passage, we note that the two blind men recognized Jesus Christ's power to heal them. They believed that this man (Jesus) could heal them, since when Jesus asks what they want, they answer that they want their eyes to be opened. Many

Christians acknowledge God's power to heal, but don't believe God wants to cure them or, worse yet, they believe that God sent them the sickness. So they don't receive healing. Notice that God has the power to heal, but He needs you to believe in the healing. In order for a miracle to occur, we need to believe; if we don't, nothing will happen because you have decided not to be healed and God respects your decision.

> *And there came a leper to Him, beseeching Him and kneeling down to Him and saying unto Him, "If Thou wilt, Thou canst make me clean." And Jesus, moved with compassion, put forth His hand and touched him, and said unto him, "I will; be thou clean." And as soon as He had spoken, immediately the leprosy departed from him, and he was cleansed.*
>
> Mark 1:40–42

Again, we find the two requirements for a miracle to occur: to recognize the power of Jesus Christ and to believe that Jesus wants to heal you.

> *And He entered again into the synagogue, and there was a man there who had a withered hand. And they watched Him to see whether He would heal him on the Sabbath day, that they might accuse Him.*
>
> Mark 3:1–2

> *And He said unto the man who had the withered hand, "Stand forth." And He said unto them, "Is it lawful to do good on the Sabbath days, or to do evil? To save life, or to kill?" But they held their peace. And when He had looked round about on them with anger, being grieved by the hardness of their hearts, He said unto the man, "Stretch forth thine hand." And he stretched it out, and his hand was restored whole as the other.*
>
> Mark 3:3–5

For He had healed many, insomuch that they pressed upon Him to touch Him, as many as had plagues.

Mark 3:10

And whithersoever He entered, into villages or cities or the country, they laid the sick in the streets, and besought Him that they might touch even the border of His garment. And as many as touched Him were made whole.

Mark 6:56

And they brought unto Him one who was deaf and had an impediment in his speech, and they besought Him to put His hand upon him. And He took him aside from the multitude and put His fingers into his ears, and He spat and touched his tongue. And looking up to Heaven, He sighed and said unto him, "Ephphatha," that is, "Be opened." And straightway his ears were opened, and the bond of his tongue was loosed and he spoke plainly. And He charged them that they should tell no man. But the more He charged them, the more widely they proclaimed it and were astonished beyond measure, saying, "He hath done all things well; he maketh both the deaf to hear and the dumb to speak."

Mark 7:32–37

And He came to Bethsaida, and they brought a blind man unto Him, and besought Him to touch him. And He took the blind man by the hand, and led him out of the town. And when He had spit on his eyes and put His hands upon him, He asked him if he saw anything. And he looked up and said, "I see men as trees, walking." After that He put His hands again upon his eyes and made him look up; and he was restored, and saw every man clearly.

Mark 8:22–25

And they came to Jericho. And as He went out of Jericho with His disciples and a great number of people, blind Bartimaeus, the son of Timaeus, sat by the wayside begging. And when he heard that it was Jesus of Nazareth, he began to cry out and say, "Jesus, Thou Son of David, have mercy on me!" And many charged him that he should hold his peace; but he cried out all the more, "Thou Son of David, have mercy on me!" And Jesus stood still, and commanded him to be called. And they called the blind man, saying unto him, "Be of good comfort; rise; He calleth thee." And he, casting away his garment, rose and came to Jesus. And Jesus answered and said unto him, "What wilt thou that I should do unto thee?" The blind man said unto Him, "Lord, that I might receive my sight." And Jesus said unto him, "Go thy way. Thy faith hath made thee whole." And immediately he received his sight, and followed Jesus in the way.

Mark 10:46–52

Now when the sun was setting, all those who had any sick with divers diseases brought them unto Him; and He laid His hands on every one of them, and healed them.

Luke 4:40

And it came to pass when He was in a certain city, behold, a man full of leprosy, seeing Jesus, fell on his face and besought Him, saying, "Lord, if Thou wilt, Thou canst make me clean." And He put forth His hand and touched him, saying, "I will: be thou clean." And immediately the leprosy departed from him.

Luke 5:12–13

And the whole multitude sought to touch Him, for there went virtue out of Him and healed them all.

Luke 6:19

And Jesus went with them. And when He was not far from the house, the centurion sent friends to Him, saying unto Him, "Lord, trouble not Thyself, for I am not worthy that Thou shouldest enter under my roof. Therefore neither thought I myself worthy to come unto Thee. But say the word, and my servant shall be healed."

Luke 7:6–7

And those who were sent, returning to the house, found the servant whole who had been sick.

Luke 7:10

And He was teaching in one of the synagogues on the Sabbath. And behold, there was a woman who had a spirit of infirmity for eighteen years, and was bowed down and could in no way lift herself up. And when Jesus saw her, He called her to Him and said unto her, "Woman, thou art loosed from thine infirmity." And He laid His hands on her, and immediately she was made straight, and glorified God.

Luke 13:10–13

And behold, there was a certain man before Him who had the dropsy. And Jesus answering, spoke unto the lawyers and Pharisees, saying, "Is it lawful to heal on the Sabbath day?" But they held their peace. And He took him and healed him, and let him go.

Luke 14:2–4

And it came to pass as He went to Jerusalem that He passed through the midst of Samaria and Galilee. And as He entered into a certain village, there met Him ten men who were lepers, who stood afar off. And they lifted up their voices and said, "Jesus, Master, have mercy on us!" And when He saw them, He said unto them, "Go, show yourselves unto the priests." And it came to pass that as they went, they were cleansed. And one of them when he saw that he was healed, turned back and with a loud voice glorified God.

Luke 17:11–15

So Jesus came again into Cana of Galilee where He had made the water wine. And there was a certain nobleman, whose son was sick at Capernaum. When he heard that Jesus had come out of Judea into Galilee, he went unto Him and besought Him that He would come down and heal his son, for he was at the point of death. Then Jesus said unto him, "Unless ye see signs and wonders, ye will not believe." The nobleman said unto Him, "Sir, come down ere my child die!" Jesus said unto him,

"Go thy way; thy son liveth." And the man believed the word that Jesus had spoken unto him, and he went his way. And as he was going down, his servants met him and told him, saying, "Thy son liveth!" Then he inquired of them the hour when he began to be healed. And they said unto him, "Yesterday at the seventh hour the fever left him." So the father knew that it was at the same hour in which Jesus had said unto him, "Thy son liveth." And he himself believed, and his whole house.

John 4:46–53

CHAPTER SIX

BE HEALED: AS YOU BELIEVE, SO IT BE DONE

And He said unto her, "Daughter, thy faith hath made thee whole. Go in peace, and be whole of thy plague."

Mark 5:35

And Jesus said unto the centurion, "Go thy way, and as thou hast believed, so be it done unto thee." And his servant was healed in that selfsame hour.

Matthew 8:13

But Jesus turned about, and when He saw her, He said, "Daughter, be of good comfort; thy faith hath made thee whole." And the woman was made whole from that hour.

Matthew 9:22

Then Jesus answered and said unto her, "O woman, great is thy faith. Be it unto thee even as thou wilt." And her daughter was made whole from that very hour.

Matthew 15:28

In this book, through the Bible, I have shown you the promises God made to you with respect to healing. We have seen how Jesus healed everyone. The power of that word is still present today: *Jesus Christ is the same yesterday, and today, and forever.* (Hebrews 13:8). God has not and will not change. The Bible says in James 1:17, *"with whom is no variableness, neither shadow of turning. God does not change."*

In Mark 13:30–1, the Word says, *"Verily I say unto you, that this generation shall not pass till all these things be done. Heaven and earth shall pass away, but My words shall not pass away."*

GOD'S WORDS
WILL NOT PASS AWAY; THEY ARE CURRENT.

You now know that the power of that word is current and that it is for you, since God does not make exceptions with people; if He did so yesterday, He will do so today.

Besides, God's word is the truth, as it says in Numbers 23:19:

God is not a man, that He should lie; neither the son of man, that He should repent. Hath He said, and shall He not do it? "I will come and heal him."

Matthew 8:7

Or hath He spoken, and shall He not make it good? He sent His word and healed them, and delivered them from their destructions.

Psalm 107:20

How does one receive healing? By hearing the Word.

But He said, "Yea rather, blessed are they that hear the Word of God and keep it."

Luke 11:28

It shall be health to thy flesh and marrow to thy bones.

Proverbs 3:8

My son, attend to my words; incline thine ear unto my sayings. Let them not depart from thine eyes, keep them in the midst of thine heart; for they are life unto those that find them and health to all their flesh.

Proverbs 4:20–22

You need faith, and you have it. And you have faith because God gave it to you; use it.

For I say to every man that is among you, through the grace given unto me, not to think of himself more highly than he ought to think, but to think soberly according as God hath dealt to every man the measure of faith.

Romans 12:3

How to receive healing:

So then faith cometh by hearing, and hearing by the Word of God.

Romans 10:17

Study and meditate on the Word day and night, like Joshua did.

This Book of the Law shall not depart out of thy mouth, but thou shalt meditate therein day and night, that thou mayest observe to do according to all that is written therein. For then thou shalt make thy way prosperous, and then THOU SHALT HAVE GOOD SUCCESS.

Joshua 1:8

How to put your faith to work—confess the Word:

But what saith it? The Word is nigh thee, even in thy mouth and in thy heart, that is, the word of faith which we preach: that if thou shalt confess with thy mouth the Lord Jesus, and shalt believe in thine heart that God hath raised Him from the dead, thou shalt be saved. For with the heart man believeth unto righteousness, and with the mouth confession is made unto salvation.

Romans 10:8–10

Confess the word—by Christ's wounds I am healed:

For the Scripture saith, WHOSOEVER BELIEVETH IN HIM SHALL NOT BE ASHAMED.

Romans 10:11

Even so faith, if it hath not works, is dead, being alone.

James 2:17

You need to say (confess) the Word and believe it, then you will receive it. Let's look at some passages of the Bible where faith brought about healing.

And when Jesus had entered into Capernaum, there came unto Him a centurion, beseeching Him and saying, "Lord, my servant lieth at home sick with the palsy and grievously tormented." And Jesus said unto him, "I will come and heal him." The centurion answered and said, "Lord, I am not worthy that Thou shouldest come under my roof. But speak the word only, and my servant shall be healed. or I am a man under authority, having soldiers under me. And I say to this man, 'Go!' and he goeth; and to another, 'Come!' and he cometh; and to my servant, 'Do this!' and he doeth it." He

> *marveled and said to those who followed, "Verily I say unto you, I have not found such great faith, no, not in Israel."*
>
> Matthew 8:5–10

> *And Jesus said unto the centurion, "Go thy way, and as thou hast believed, so be it done unto thee." And his servant was healed in that selfsame hour.*
>
> Matthew 8:13

The centurion believed Him and confessed his belief. And you know what? He received.

And to the woman who bled (Mark 5:34), He said, "*Daughter, thy faith hath made thee whole. Go in peace, and be whole of thy plague*" (Mark 5:34). To the leper who returned cleansed, He said, *"Go thy way. Thy faith hath made thee whole" (*Luke 17:19). And Jesus said to Jairus, *"DO NOT FEAR, ONLY BELIEVE."*

To the blind man in Jericho, Jesus said unto him, *"Go thy way. Thy faith hath made thee whole"* (Luke 18:42) To the father whose son was possessed by demons, *Jesus said unto him, "If thou canst believe, all things are possible to him that believeth"* (Mark 9:23).

> *And Jesus, looking upon them, said, "With men it is impossible, but not with God; FOR WITH GOD ALL THINGS ARE POSSIBLE."*
>
> Mark 10:27

What did Jesus say?

THAT ALL, ALL THINGS ARE POSSIBLE FOR GOD. SO IF YOU BELIEVE HIS WORD AND CONFESS IT, YOU WILL RECEIVE HEALING, ALTHOUGH IT MAY SEEM IMPOSSIBLE.

For with God nothing shall be impossible.

Luke 1:37

What you need is faith the size of a grain of mustard seed, which is very, very small.

For verily I say unto you, if ye have faith as a grain of mustard seed, ye shall say unto this mountain, "Remove hence to yonder place," and it shall remove. And nothing shall be impossible unto you.

Matthew 17:20

God says in His Word:

AND WHATSOEVER YE SHALL ASK IN MY NAME, THAT WILL I DO, THAT THE FATHER MAY BE GLORIFIED IN THE SON.

John 14:13

By using the powerful name of Jesus you receive healing.

If ye shall ask anything in My name, I will do it.

John 14:14

Do all in the name of the Lord Jesus.

Colossians 3:17

Take the name of Jesus and you will be healed. In the name of Jesus, I declare myself healed. Amen.

Jesus answered and said unto them, "Verily I say unto you, if ye have faith and doubt not, ye shall not only do this which is done to the fig tree, but also if ye shall say unto this mountain, 'Be thou removed and be thou cast into the sea,' it shall be done."

Matthew 21:21

AND ALL things whatsoever ye shall ask in prayer, believing, ye shall receive.

Matthew 21:22

Jesus answered and said unto them, "Have faith in God. For verily I say unto you,

that whosoever shall say unto this mountain, 'Be thou removed, and be thou cast into the sea,' and shall not doubt in his heart, but shall believe that those things which he saith shall come to pass, he shall have whatsoever he saith."

Mark 11:22–23

The Word says that everything you say in belief, without doubt, will be done. In other words, if you declare yourself healed in the name of Jesus, you will be healed.

Therefore I say unto you, what things so ever ye desire when ye pray, believe that ye receive them, and ye shall have them.

Mark 11:24

EVERYTHING I ASK FOR BY PRAYING AND BELIEVING, I WILL RECEIVE;

IT WILL COME TO ME.

Ask, and it shall be given you; seek, and ye shall find; knock, and it shall be opened unto you. For every one that asketh receiveth; and he that seeketh findeth; and to him that knocketh it shall be opened. Or what man is there among you whom, if his son ask for bread, will give him a stone? Or if he asks for a fish, will give him a serpent? If ye then, being evil, know how to give good gifts unto your children, how much more shall your Father who is in Heaven give good things to them that ask Him?

Matthew 7:7–11

Health is a good thing, so receive it. Moreover, God gave us the greatest thing of all before we asked: His Son.

He that spared not His own Son, but delivered Him up for us all, how shall He not with Him also freely give us all things?

Romans 8:32

And the whole multitude sought to touch Him, for there went virtue out of Him and healed them all.

Luke 6:19

That power continues to flow through believers. You can touch that garment through your prayer for healing, since God gave believers the power and authority to heal. They shall lay hands on the sick, and they shall recover.

Mark 16:18

So when your laying of hands as a believer occurs, you are touching Jesus' healing garment as in the days that He walked the earth. Receive, then, your healing. Christ is willing to heal you; you only need to believe, because "*all things are possible to him that believeth"* (Mark 9:23); *" believe that ye receive them, and ye shall have them"* (Mark 11:24).

> *But say the word, and my servant shall be healed.*
>
> Luke 7:7

Say the word: "By His wounds we have been healed." You are healed in the name of Jesus. I am healed.

> *But He was wounded for our transgressions; He was bruised for our iniquities. The chastisement of our peace was upon Him, and with His stripes we are healed.*
>
> Isaiah 53:5

And by His wounds we were healed, that is God's promise and God's word, and it has been done, as it is in the past tense; it does not say you will be healed, but that before we came to this world, God had paid the price for sickness. Before you were born, God had paid the price so that you could walk in a healthy body. Jesus paid the price.

> *Now there is in Jerusalem by the sheep market a pool, which is called in the Hebrewtongue Bethesda, having five porches. In these lay a great multitude of invalid folk — blind, halt, withered — waiting for the moving of the water. An angel went down at a certain season into the pool and troubled the water. Whosoever then first stepped in, after the troubling of the water, was made whole of whatsoever disease he had. And a certain man was there who had an infirmity for thirty and eight years.*
>
> *When Jesus saw him lying there, and knew that he had been in that state a long time, He said unto him, "Wilt thou be made*

whole?" The infirm man answered Him, "Sir, I have no man, when the water is troubled, to put me into the pool; but while I am coming, another steppeth down before me."

John 5:2–7

The man had not recognized the power of God, and he was focused on his illness and on the limitation that no man could help him enter the pool.

Jesus said unto him, "Rise, take up thy bed, and walk."

John 5:8

Jesus did not reprimand or argue with him saying He could heal him. He did not even say who He was. He simply healed him. Let's look at this:

And immediately the man was made whole, and took up his bed and walked. Now it was the Sabbath on that day.

John 5:9

And his health was immediate, but not all healing occurs instantly. Sometimes health manifests itself little by little in a process of healing. The important thing is to believe. Once the prayer for healing has been said, the person will receive health at that moment, although it may take a while to manifest itself. The person will continue to confess that, by Christ's wounds, *I AM HEALED*. Amen

HEALING IN THE BIBLE

For I am the Lord that healeth thee.

Exodus 15:26

And I will take sickness away from the midst of thee.

Exodus 23:25

Behold, I will bring it health and cure; and I will cure them.

Jeremiah 33:6

...who healeth all thy diseases.

Psalm 103:3

And there was not one feeble person among their tribes.

Psalm 105:37

He sent His word and healed them, and delivered them from their destructions.

Psalm 107:20

Then they cried unto the Lord in their trouble, and He delivered them out of their distresses.

Psalm 107:6

And as many as touched Him were made whole.

Mark 6:56

But say the word, and my servant shall be healed.

Luke 7:7

Beloved, I wish above all things that thou mayest prosper and be in health, even as thy soul prospereth.

3 John 1:2

And Jesus put forth His hand and touched him, saying, ***I will; be thou clean****. And immediately his leprosy was cleansed.*

Matthew 8:3

PRAYER IN AGREEMENT FOR HEALING

Again I say unto you, that if two of you shall agree on earth concerning anything that they shall ask, it shall be done for them by My Father who is in Heaven. For where two or three are gathered together in My name, there am I in the midst of them.

Matthew 18:19–20

Father, I am in agreement with
Carmen Betancourt, You know my need.
We come before You and declare
your healing word.
By your wounds we were healed;
you paid the price for this illness or condition.
Father, I believe in Your word.
I believe in Christ's sacrifice on the cross.
I ask Your forgiveness for all my sins,
I accept you as my Lord and Savior,
please come into my life.
And now, Father, in the powerful name of Jesus
I declare divine life and health in my body,
I receive Your healing.
I stand firm in my confession
of Your healing word in me.
Thank you, Father, for it is done.
Amen.

Now, brother or sister, receive your healing, as the Bible says that if two or more people agree on anything they ask for, it shall be done by our Father, who is in heaven. So glorify God and give Him thanks, praise Him and share your testimony with others of what God has done for you.

If you have yet to make Christ your Lord and Savior, pray:

PRAYER TO ACCEPT CHRIST AS YOUR LORD AND SAVIOR

I come before you to declare that You are my Lord;

please forgive all my sins and

make me a new creature

who will serve and adore you.

From here on

I promise to live for you.
Thank you, Father, for receiving me.

Amen.

If you wish, you may write to me at the following email:
jesus_sana@hotmail.com

God bless you.

Lightning Source UK Ltd.
Milton Keynes UK
UKHW022125080223
416726UK00021B/319

9 798887 384214